SAM  RATE

# THE
# TREASURE MAP

*Collect all the* Sam Silver: Undercover Pirate *books*

❏ Skeleton Island

❏ The Ghost Ship

❏ Kidnapped

❏ The Deadly Trap

❏ Dragon Fire

❏ The Double-cross

❏ The Great Rescue

☑ The Treasure Map

# THE
# TREASURE MAP

Jan Burchett and Sara Vogler

*Illustrated by Leo Hartas*

Orion
Children's Books

First published in Great Britain in 2013
by Orion Children's Books
a division of the Orion Publishing Group Ltd
Orion House
5 Upper St Martin's Lane
London WC2H 9EA
An Hachette UK company

1 3 5 7 9 10 8 6 4 2

A catalogue record for this book is available from the British Library.

ISBN 978 1 4440 0764 0

Printed in Great Britain by Clays Ltd, St Ives plc

For Kirsty, Kerry, Sue and Lyle Elliott.

N
CUBA
TORTUGA
Puerto Caballo
HISPANIOLA
Montego Bay
JAMAICA
Cloud of Death
CARIBBEAN

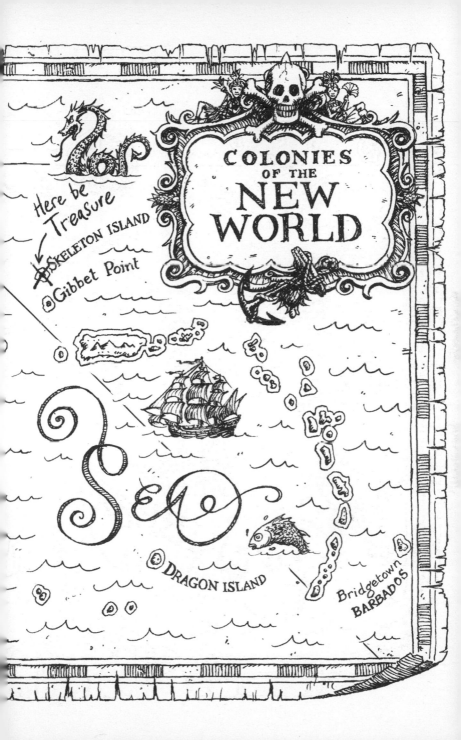

The SEA WOLF

Captain's Cabin
Hammocks
Gun Deck
Galley
Ship's Stores

# CHAPTER ONE

Sam Silver stood in front of his class and held up his ancient gold doubloon. Their teacher had asked them to bring in the oldest thing they could find for their history lesson, and his coin was three hundred years old. If that wasn't history, then what was?

"This is a Double Eagle doubloon," said Sam eagerly. "It's really ancient and it used to belong to my great-great-lots-of-greats-grandfather, who was a pirate."

There was a gasp from the class but Sam could see his teacher looking doubtful.

"Did your parents tell you that?" asked Miss Elliott.

"No," said Sam. "It got washed up on the beach in a bottle, but I know it belongs to my family because there was a letter with it that explained everything."

Someone tittered near the back.

"It's true," insisted Sam. "I know because . . ." He stopped. He realised he couldn't tell the class anything else about his special coin. There was no way he was going to let out the doubloon's great secret — that it could whisk him back in time to the decks of the pirate ship *Sea Wolf* where he served as lookout boy under Captain Blade, the boldest buccaneer to sail the Caribbean Sea. Time-travelling undercover pirates can't tell anyone about their plundering adventures.

"Because?" prompted Miss Elliott.

"Er . . ." Sam said at last, feeling a bit embarrassed. "That's all I can say."

"Well, it's the oldest object today," said his teacher kindly. The bell rang for the end of school. "Homework, everyone!" she called over its chimes. "You brought in some very interesting historical items and now you're going to write stories about them. I want you to imagine you're living back in the time of your object."

Sam raced home to the flat above his parents' shop – The Jolly Cod, Best Fish and Chips in Backwater Bay. He'd had a great idea. He bounded up the stairs to his bedroom, threw off his school uniform and pulled on his tattiest T-shirt and jeans. Then he tipped the coin out of his backpack. He was going to have some pirate fun with his friends back in 1706. After that he could write it all up for homework and not even miss tea. That was the clever thing about the doubloon. No time ever passed in the present when he was off buccaneering.

He spat on the coin and rubbed it hard on his sleeve. "*Sea Wolf*, here I come!" he declared.

He felt the room begin to spin. The next moment he was pulled off his feet and tumbled round and round as if he'd been hoovered up in a giant vacuum cleaner. He braced himself for the landing. *Bump!* He was sitting on the wooden floor of a little storeroom, which was gently rocking. Awesome! He was back on the *Sea Wolf*.

Sam scrambled to his feet and gathered up the belt, jerkin, spyglass and neckerchief lying in the corner. His pirate friend, Charlie, always put them ready for him. She was the only other person in the world who knew that he was a time traveller – she'd seen him appear out of thin air once so he'd had to tell her the truth. It had taken some explaining but she'd understood, and now she helped to keep his secret.

Eager to see his crewmates, Sam sprang up the steps to the main deck and burst out into the hot Caribbean sunshine. The ship was moored in a bustling port where men were carrying crates and rolling

barrels along the quay. There was an
unpleasant smell of rotting fish wafting
across the ship. To his surprise the *Sea Wolf*
seemed empty. He felt a shiver of worry.
Where were his crewmates? Then a deep
voice hailed him from the foredeck.

"By the Great Bear, it's Sam Silver!" A
tall pirate in a tricorn hat was leaning over
the rail above him, weapons gleaming in
the belts across his chest. His bearded face
was wreathed in smiles.

"Captain Blade!" exclaimed Sam in relief. "Where is everybody?"

"Shore leave, lad," the captain called down. "Well, all except Peter. He's in the galley doing some cooking. The last fish pies he made were so hard we could have used them in the cannon. I thought he'd better stay on board and practise his pastry."

Sam realised that the nasty smell was coming from the galley, the ship's kitchen. He was glad he wasn't hungry. Even if Peter practised for a whole year he'd never produce anything that didn't break your teeth or send you running for the sick bucket.

"Permission to go ashore and find the others," said Sam eagerly.

"Surely you must have seen them when you came through the town," said Blade, puzzled. "Puerto Nuevo's not that big a place."

"Er . . . well . . . the thing is . . ." said Sam, racking his brains for an excuse. He couldn't tell the captain that he hadn't come through the town at all, but simply popped up in the storeroom from three hundred years in the future.

Every time Sam disappeared from the *Sea Wolf* to go back to the present, the crew believed that he'd gone to help his poor widowed mother on her farm, somewhere in the Caribbean. But he never remembered to have an excuse ready when he appeared on board without warning. And this time Charlie wasn't around to come to his rescue.

"I was in such a hurry to be with you all again," he said at last, "that I kept my eyes fixed on the ship."

"Well go and find your shipmates now," said Blade, ushering him towards the gangplank. "You've got time before we set sail."

"Thank you," said Sam, relieved that the captain wasn't asking any more questions.

"Ahoy, me hearty!" came a squawk. A green parrot landed on his shoulder and began to nibble his ear.

"Hello, Crow," said Sam, tickling him under his beak. "Did you miss me?"

"You can take that . . . bird with you," said the captain shakily.

Captain Blade was the bravest man

Sam had ever met — except when he was faced with a parrot. Charlie had heard it was because a parrot had pinched his toy cutlass when he was little, but all the pirates had different tales to tell. Everyone knew to keep the parrot away from Blade and pretend it was an unusually colourful crow.

"Aye, aye," said Sam smartly. He bounded down onto the quay and scanned the crowd, looking for Charlie and their friend, Fernando.

He walked past shops and taverns, skirting the fishing nets and lobster pots strewn over the cobbles. There was no sign of Charlie's bright bandana or Fernando's dark curly hair. Sam was willing to bet that most of the men he could see were pirates like them, who were acting like ordinary sailors but ready to vanish in an instant if the governor's soldiers came by. Then he spotted Harry

Hopp, the *Sea Wolf's* first mate, sitting at
a table outside one of the taverns. Harry
was playing cards, a tankard at his elbow
and his wooden leg stuck out in front of
him. A scrawny-looking man sat opposite
him, his cards clutched secretively to his
chest. Sam was about to call his shipmate's
name when Harry jumped up, knocking
his stool flying.

"Stormy seas?" squawked Crow, tucking his head into Sam's jerkin.

"Looks like it," said Sam as Harry pushed the table over, sending tankards and cards into the air.

Harry launched himself at the scrawny man and dragged him to his feet. "I won fair and square!" he yelled, a thunderous look on his face. "Pay up now or it's the last game you'll ever play."

# CHAPTER TWO

A crowd was gathering round the two men. Voices were rising and Sam could hear the sounds of a fight. He was pushing his way through to discover what was going on when he heard someone exclaim in Spanish. He turned to see Fernando behind him, his eyes bright with excitement.

"My friend!" Fernando had a broad

grin on his face. "Where did you spring from?"

"The captain told me you were all in town," said Sam, "so I came to see what you were up to."

"You're just in time," said a voice at his side. Charlie was standing there, looking every inch a pirate deckhand with her bare feet and ragged boy's trousers. "We've got to stop Harry fighting and get him back to the ship."

"But I want to watch what happens," Fernando went on eagerly. "He's boiling up like one of Peter's stews."

"I hope he doesn't smell as bad," laughed Sam.

"It's not funny!" insisted Charlie as the shouts grew louder. "Harry might do something silly and get the governor's men on to us. Follow me."

They elbowed their way to the front of the jostling mob who were urging the two men on. Tables, chairs and tankards littered the ground and the cobbles were sticky with spilt drink. Harry Hopp had his opponent backed against the tavern wall. His stubbly face was bright red with fury and the scrawny man was cowering. One eye rolled with fear but the other stayed still, staring straight ahead. It was shiny, with a bright blue iris and gold round the edge. *It's a false eye*, thought Sam with surprise. He'd seen a pirate in a film with one once but that had been wooden. This one looked as if it was made of painted glass. It was amazing – and a bit creepy.

"You told me you had money to pay," growled Harry, nose to nose with the one-eyed man.

The man gulped, white-faced. "I . . . I . . . thought I was going to win," he managed to croak.

"Don't believe 'im," shouted someone

from the crowd. "That Scammell's always been a slippery cove! He's running a rig!"

Sam knew enough pirate talk to know what that meant. Harry's opponent had been trying to con him.

"You cod-faced bilge drinker!" Harry's hand flew to his belt and suddenly he was holding a knife to his captive's throat. "If you don't cough up the money you'll be coughing up your life's blood instead."

"Down among the dead men!" squawked Crow.

"We must stop this," hissed Charlie.

"I can pay!" Scammell was squealing as he writhed away from the blade. "I ain't got coins but I 'ave got something you'll want. I'll show you."

Harry stared at him for a moment. Then he took the knife from the man's throat, keeping a grasp on one arm.

Scammell slowly reached into the pocket of his shabby coat and produced a scroll of paper, tied with greasy string. "This is worth much more than I owe you," he said, "but it's all I've got."

Harry tightened his grip on the man's sleeve. "What is this parchment that it's so valuable?" he demanded.

"It was given to me by my old friend, Jake Haskins, as he lay dying," croaked

Scammell, his real eye darting from side to side in panic. "I never thought to part with it but needs must. It's a map that will lead you to a great hoard of treasure. This is the only copy in the world. Plenty of booty for you and all your crew."

# CHAPTER THREE

Sam felt a thrill run through him. A treasure map sounded really exciting.

But Harry's face hardened again. "I've only got your word for that," he said angrily. "Perhaps I should slit your throat after all."

Charlie leapt forwards and caught the first mate's sleeve. "I don't think that's a good idea," she said urgently.

"That scurvy seadog's not worth bloodying your knife for, Mr Hopp," Fernando called. "And, who knows, he could be right about the map."

Harry gave a disgusted snort and, loosening his grip on Scammell, yanked open the yellowed parchment. "We'll soon see about that." He cast a quick glance at it. "This is useless," he roared. "It's just a lot of spidery lines, and most of those have faded away! You—"

A cry went up from the quayside. "Governor's men! Coming this way."

Before Harry could stop him, Scammell had slipped off among the fleeing drinkers.

"I've been cheated," growled Harry. He crumpled the map and threw it angrily to the ground.

"Back to the ship, everyone!" urged Charlie.

Sam wasn't going to leave a treasure map behind. He grabbed it and dashed after

Charlie towards the *Sea Wolf*. He could hear Harry Hopp's angry muttering and his peg leg clattering on the cobbles. The rest of the crew came streaming out of the tavern, making for the ship.

As the pirates pulled the gangplank up behind them, Ben Hudson, the quartermaster, looked back towards the inn. "That's odd," he panted. "I can't see any soldiers."

Sam realised Ben was right. Now everyone had stopped running, the town was returning to its normal bustle and there wasn't a governor's man in sight.

"Better to be safe than sorry," said Charlie.

"Yes, my friend," agreed Fernando. "We don't want to end up dangling from the hangman's rope!"

"What's going on?" demanded Captain Blade, striding across the deck. "You've got a face like an angry haddock, Harry."

"Mr Hopp won a treasure map in a card game," explained Charlie.

"It was useless," growled Harry. "I threw it away."

"But I saved it!" Sam pulled the map from his pocket and spread it out on the deck.

The crew gathered round and peered at it. Sam was surprised. He'd expected to see islands, trees and an X marking the spot, but this square parchment was covered in strange wiggly lines that seemed to make no sense.

"Well, I'll be a rat in a rum barrel!" exclaimed Ned Wainwright. "That's no treasure map."

"Looks more like the veins on my hand," agreed Ben.

"Or dead worms," added Peter, peering at the paper.

"I said it was useless!" snapped Harry. "If I ever get hold of that . . ."

But Sam was staring intently at the strange wiggly lines on the parchment. They were brown and faded but they reminded him of something.

"Potholing!" he exclaimed suddenly. He remembered someone coming into school dressed up like a miner and telling them all about his adventures in caves. He'd shown them how to follow a potholer's map and then they'd made their own. It had been awesome.

He realised that the crew were looking at him as if he'd grown horns.

"What's he talking about?" asked Peter suspiciously. "He's not going to make holes in my pots, is he?"

"Of course not," said Sam. He should have realised that eighteenth-century pirates didn't know anything about potholing. He wondered how he was going to get out of this one.

"Potholing is something your mum knows all about, isn't it, Sam?" prompted Charlie, giving him a nudge.

"That's right," said Sam, thankful that his friend had come to his rescue. "She's always exploring caves – and she calls it potholing because . . . she wears a pot on her head in case the cave falls in on her. Anyway, this looks just like the cave maps she takes with her. See, there's a route marked out in a faded brown line and the entrance seems to be in some sort of inlet. That squiggle there could be a bit of coast and that X marks the treasure."

"But we still don't know where in the world it is," sniffed Harry Hopp.

Captain Blade snatched the map and examined it. "There's something written here but it's very faint," he said. "'These caves be on the southern shore of Isla Cocoza'," he read slowly. "By the stars, the boy's right! This map does show caves. We've all heard of the Caves of Cocoza and the great riches hidden there. Well done, lad."

Sam felt a huge grin spread across his face. Soon they'd be setting sail on a treasure hunt.

Harry stamped his wooden leg on the deck. "And we've all heard what happens to those who go in after those riches!" he spat. "That scurvy rat knew we'd never venture near the place any more than he would. I should have slit his throat and fed him to the sharks."

"But surely we're going to hunt for this treasure!" said Sam.

The crew shook their heads.

"You must have heard of the terrible Caves of Cocoza," said Captain Blade.

"Didn't your mother warn you about them?" asked Ben. "She's a cave expert, after all."

Sam shook his head. The pirates looked at him in disbelief.

"Sam told me his mum has a terrible memory for names," said Charlie helpfully.

"That's right," agreed Sam. "She's always mixing me up with the cow."

"It doesn't matter a jot," shouted Harry Hopp. "What does matter is that I've been cheated by that hornswoggler."

Sam couldn't believe the crew were going to turn their back on such a prize. "Do we have to forget about the booty then?"

"It's no good to us if we never see the light of day with it," said Ned, "like all those that have gone before."

"But they didn't have a map," insisted

Sam. "We do. I can find the way easily."

Some of the crew looked hopeful at this but others muttered among themselves.

Captain Blade slapped Sam on the back. "The lad's right," he declared. "We have a map. I say we set sail for the Caves of Cocoza right away."

Harry Hopp stood with his arms folded, scowling. Then his eyes began to sparkle. "We *do* have a Silver on board with his Silver's luck," he said.

The superstitious pirates, who were convinced that Sam brought them good fortune, gave a rousing cheer.

"That's true," declared Ned. "Sam led us to Skeleton Island and its treasure."

"And he got the better of Blackheart and his dastardly men," added Ben.

"What are we waiting for?" demanded Harry Hopp. "Let's have a treasure hunt."

"Aye!" cried the crew.

# CHAPTER FOUR

Sam stood in the crow's nest, the wind whipping his hair. He was on lookout with Crow on his shoulder, who squawked bossily at any seagulls that came too near. Sam was scanning the water for the first glimpse of the mysterious Isla Cocoza. Captain Blade had told him it was a rugged island with high, jagged peaks.

"Any sign of land?" Harry shouted up to him from his place at the wheel.

"Not yet, Mr Hopp," Sam yelled down, "but there's a ship far to the west." Sam knew he must always report passing ships – any one of them could be a pirate vessel or the governor's men coming after the *Sea Wolf*.

The captain pointed his spyglass over the starboard bow. "She won't be heading for Cocoza, I'll warrant," he called. "No one in their right mind goes there." He chuckled. "Unless they have a treasure map."

Sam swung his gaze round the horizon again. His stomach knotted at the thought of the dangerous adventure ahead – if they ever found the island! The sea stretched out before him, blue and empty, little white flecks foaming on the swell of the waves. There was no land on any side.

"Ahoy, you lazy lubber!" came a voice
and Fernando appeared on the yardarm
just below Sam's position. He scrambled
along it, grumbling as he tightened a loose
rope. "Someone didn't fasten this sheet
properly. It's all right for you. You've got
the easy job today!"

Sam grinned. "Easy?" he said.
"Anyone can climb up and down the
rigging, but it takes a good eye and a
lot of concentration to be on lookout.
Don't you worry — as soon as there's
an island to see, I'll be the first to see
it."

"Is that right, my friend?" chuckled
Fernando, gazing over Sam's shoulder.
"So I'm just imagining that funny-looking
thing dead ahead then."

"Land ahoy!" said Crow helpfully.

Sam whirled round. Fernando was right.
A tiny speck in the distance was growing
bigger by the minute. He whipped out

his spyglass and a small barren island
appeared.

"I would have seen it first if you hadn't
been chatting," he insisted as Fernando
laughed. "Isla Cocoza dead ahead!" he
shouted down.

"Keep a straight course!" they heard
Harry Hopp order the crew.

Sam brought the island into sharp focus.

"It looks a bit creepy," he muttered to his friend, handing the spyglass over.

Fernando trained it on the island and gave a low whistle. "Creepy indeed. They say the caves are guarded by strange winged creatures. They are neither bird nor beast and they have a screech as shrill as a banshee's."

"Ready to go about," called the captain. "We're heading for the south shore."

Fernando swung down the rigging to help trim the sails.

Soon the *Sea Wolf* was racing through the wild waves along the southern coastline. The island looked just as unfriendly close up. The rocks rose steeply to jagged points, black against the blue sky. Sheer ridges swept up from the sea like giant eagle wings. His heart pounding with excitement, Sam scoured the cliffs for signs of an inlet.

"This is going to be scary," he told Crow. "I'd better keep a weather eye out for those creatures Fernando was talking about."

Suddenly there were loud cries from overhead.

"Enemy attack!" screeched the parrot, flapping his wings in alarm.

Sam looked up fearfully, expecting the sky to be full of flying monsters. Instead he caught sight of a gang of gulls, circling above the masts.

"You can come out, Crow," he said in relief. "We're not in any danger — except from their poo!"

He went back to his search but he could see they were nearly at the eastern headland with open sea beyond. They were running out of island!

"I knew it was a trick." Harry was pounding round the deck, waving the map in the air. "That fiend's sent us on a wild-goose chase. The only thing this is good for is to stoke the galley fire!"

Sam scanned the shore intently. The caves had to be here somewhere. And he had to find them before Harry burnt the map.

Then he spotted a gap in the rocks, leading to what looked like a narrow inlet. He strained to see what lay at its far end. He could make out a dark hole. That must be the place! It was the same shape as the one on the map. But Harry was already at the galley door. Sam had to stop him.

"Wait!" he yelled at the top of his voice. "I've found the caves!"

# CHAPTER FIVE

Harry stopped in his tracks and looked in the direction of Sam's pointing finger.

"The lad's right!" exclaimed Captain Blade. "Silver's luck saves the day again."

Harry hastily pocketed the map.

"Let's get at that treasure!" shouted Fernando.

"Drop anchor," ordered the captain.

"We'll hole the *Sea Wolf* if we go any closer to those rocks. We'll take a rowing boat."

Sam's whole body fizzed with excitement as he climbed down the rigging to join the crew. Crow fluttered after him, landing on his shoulder as soon as he got to the deck.

Sails flapped loose and were quickly brought down and furled. Sam heard the grinding of the anchor's metal chain being played out over the side and he felt the *Sea Wolf* slow. He ran to join Fernando and Charlie, who were helping to lower the rowing boat. As soon as it hit the water there was a streak of black fur and Sinbad, the ship's surly cat, leapt aboard, ran to the bows and plonked himself down like a scruffy figurehead.

"I hope the captain says we can go ashore," said Sam eagerly. "It's OK for Sinbad. No one would dare to stop him."

Fernando nodded. Sinbad would fight for any member of the *Sea Wolf's* crew but only Charlie was allowed to touch him.

"You will certainly be with us in the party, Sam," said Captain Blade, striding to the rail, "though you'd better leave that . . . crow on board."

"Thank you, sir!" said Sam, coaxing the parrot onto a barrel

"Danger ahead!" squawked Crow.

"You're a bit of an expert with an underground map," the captain went on, "or at least your mother is. Let's hope she taught you well."

"She certainly did," said Sam fervently. He couldn't tell the crew that the nearest his mum ever came to cave exploring was when she had to go down into their cellar. And then she always came up yelling if she met a spider. "But can Charlie and Fernando come too?"

"Aye," said Blade. "You're all small and nimble. Just what we want."

"Don't forget me!" declared Harry. "It's my map. I'm not missing the fun."

Sam was the first to jump out of the rowing boat and clamber over the slippery rocks up to the black hole of the cave. The rock above hung in jagged points like the teeth of a monster. It made him think of the shark's-mouth entrance to the Sensational Sea Centre in Backwater Bay. When he was little his dad had had to remind him that the vicious-looking teeth were only made of plastic and weren't going to eat him.

Charlie was close behind. "It's a bit scary," she said in a tiny voice. Her words echoed round the rocks in a strange whisper.

Sam fought down the fears that were creeping into his brain at the sight of the dark, unwelcoming cave. He watched as Sinbad padded in, sat down in the middle and started to clean his ears.

"If Sinbad thinks it's OK, we needn't worry," he said, trying to sound as if he didn't have a care in the world.

"And we have lights," said Fernando, holding up two lanterns.

Harry Hopp was slipping some sacks into his belt. "We'll fill these with the booty and go back again if we can't carry it all." He tied a couple of water bottles beside them, then pulled the map from inside his shirt and studied it, a frown on his grizzled face. He handed it to Sam. "You should have this, lad," he said. "I can't make head nor tail of the thing."

Sam looked at the faded ink. "There's a tunnel leading off from the back of the cave," he told his companions.

"Then we'll follow it," said Blade, holding a lantern to light the way. "Are you ready?"

"Aye!" cried Sam and his friends.

"Lead me to it!" declared Harry.

As soon as they were out of the sunlight the air felt cold on their skin. The cave narrowed into a twisting passage with a very low roof. Even Charlie had to bend her head. Sinbad stalked silently along in front of them. The jagged walls caught at their clothes and scratched their arms.

"The tunnel forks here," called Captain Blade. "Which way, Sam?"

"Keep to the left," said Sam, tracing the route with his finger.

They followed the twists and turns of the passage, climbing over rough boulders which almost blocked the path. Sometimes the roof was so low that they were forced to go on all fours. Sam slid the map into his jeans pocket. He needed both hands free to keep his balance.

"We must be deep inside the island now," whispered Charlie, crawling along behind him. "I've never been anywhere like this before."

"Me neither," said Sam.

The passage widened into an eerie cave. Long pointed columns of rock hung over their heads and others rose up from the ground to meet them.

"Stalactites and stalagmites," announced Sam. "It's where water has dissolved some of the rock and it's dripped down." He glanced at the astonished faces of the pirates. "My mum told me," he went on quickly. "She only remembers which is which because stalac*tites* hold *tight* to the roof and stalag*mites* stand *mighty* on the ground!"

"You've got a *mighty* lot of learning for one so young," laughed Harry Hopp. "I've never heard them called stally-whatsits. How about you, Fernando?"

But Fernando wasn't listening. He was pointing a wobbly finger at the roof.

"What's that?" he whispered.

Sam followed his terrified gaze. There was something moving between the stalactites. Something black that covered the ceiling and writhed and squirmed.

# CHAPTER SIX

As they watched, a dark shape with jagged leathery wings broke away from the seething mass. It swooped through the cave, casting huge, terrifying shadows in the lantern light.

Charlie scooped Sinbad into her arms and hid her face in his fur. "What is it?" she wailed.

"It must be one of the guardians of the

cave!" gasped Harry. "What else can it be?"

"Neither bird nor beast," muttered Fernando in a horrified whisper. "The stories were true."

Sam found himself shivering and he knew it wasn't just from the cold.

*Merow!* Using Charlie's shoulder as a launchpad, Sinbad sprang towards the roof, yowling and swiping with his long claws.

At once the air was full of shrill, whistling cries and thousands of winged creatures swooped straight at them. Charlie pressed herself against the cave wall, covering her ears to block out the dreadful sound.

The thought slipped into Sam's brain that he'd seen things like these before but, at that moment, Sinbad hurtled into him. Sam went tumbling onto the hard rock floor, the cat gripping tightly to his jeans.

"We must leave this place," cried Harry. "They don't want us here."

"Too late," groaned Fernando, covering his head. "They'll never let us escape."

"Hush your noise!" barked Captain Blade. "Is anyone hurt?"

"No, Captain."

"And you won't be, either." The captain held up his lantern. "These are no monsters — they're just bats."

Sam got to his feet and stared hard at the sinister shapes. So that's why they'd seemed familiar. He'd heard the high-pitched calls of bats and spotted them flitting about when he'd been out in the dark in Backwater Bay. But here in this gloomy cave he'd been too spooked to see what was in front of his eyes – and these were a lot bigger than any of the bats he'd ever met!

The bats circled the cave, swooping and soaring. One of them suddenly landed on Sam, making him jump with surprise. It hung upside down from his jerkin, and peered at him with round, nervous eyes before taking off again to join the others. At last the whole colony settled back under the cave roof, where they chittered softly.

Harry Hopp gave a low chuckle. "Stap me!" he exclaimed. "No wonder there were so many scary stories! These bats are giants compared to those I've seen before. They'd frighten many a man into running for his life."

"Poor things," said Sam. "Sinbad disturbed their sleep. They shouldn't be awake until they go hunting at night. I remember that from the telly . . . I mean, I remember my mum *telling* me."

"Your mother certainly knows a lot!" said Harry, impressed.

Fernando was shining his lantern round the walls on the other side. "There's two ways out here," he called. "What does the map say?"

Sam studied the route. "It's the right-hand one," he called back. "The other's a dead end."

"Lead the way, Fernando," said the captain. "We'll be right behind you."

The pirates made their way through the forest of stalagmites. Sinbad strutted at Charlie's feet, growling deep in his throat.

"Poor boy!" she crooned. "Did those naughty creatures scare you?" Sam smiled to himself. The baleful ship's cat looked anything but scared.

At that moment a massive bat came zooming from the roof. It swept past Sinbad's nose and flew up to disappear through a hole high in the wall. In an instant Sinbad was making for the hole,

claws scraping on the stone. Before Charlie could stop him he'd vanished from sight. The sounds of his chase became fainter and fainter until they couldn't hear him any more.

"Sinbad!" yelled Charlie, climbing after him.

"Avast ye!" ordered Blade, pulling her back to the ground. "You don't know where that leads."

"But neither does Sinbad!" wailed Charlie.

"He'll join us when he's ready." Blade's tone was kinder now. "*We* might need a map but he'll know where he's going."

"Aye." Harry Hopp grinned. "He's a canny cat."

"But—" Charlie began.

"We'll find him before we leave," Fernando assured her. "We'd never abandon a crew member." He took her hand. "You and I will go first," he said, leading her into the tunnel. "I bet Sinbad will meet us at the other end."

They hadn't gone far when Harry Hopp called them to a halt. "What's that sound?" he asked. They could all hear it now – a deep pounding noise somewhere ahead.

"Water," said Blade. "I'll warrant there's an underground river around here."

Soon the lanterns lit up a fast-running stream that gushed out of a hole in the rock, spilling along the tunnel in front of them and flowing rapidly away into the dark.

"That map never told us we had to swim!" grumbled the first mate.

Blade tested the depth. The water didn't rise above his knees. "Just a bit of paddling, Harry. But be cautious, everybody. It's a strong flow and the going's slippery on these rocks."

The icy water made Sam gasp as he stepped into the stream.

Holding the lanterns high, the pirates waded along, clutching the walls for support.

"I hope Sinbad doesn't come this way," said Charlie anxiously.

Sam felt the river gradually deepening. The water seeped up his jeans. Then he remembered the map in his pocket. Quickly he pulled it out. It was still dry! He held it over his head to stop it being splashed and struggled on, trying to stay upright against the force of the water. The river was over his waist now. Suddenly he stumbled and his feet were swooshed away from under him. He felt a shock of icy cold closing over his head. The river rushed in his ears as he desperately tried to find his footing. He needed to breathe, but he couldn't get to the surface. He was being tumbled against the rocks.

He felt someone grasp him firmly and he was dragged up into the air by strong arms. Harry Hopp was grinning down at him.

"This is no time for hide-and-seek!" the first mate chuckled. "You had us worried there, lad."

But Sam couldn't answer. He stared

glumly at his empty hands. He'd lost the map. Now they would never find the treasure.

# CHAPTER SEVEN

"You might be needing this, my friend!"

Dazed, Sam shook the water from his eyes. Fernando was holding something out. It was the map!

"How . . ." began Sam.

"Simple," said Fernando, with a wicked grin. "Your hand clutching the map was the last thing to disappear. I reckoned that even if you perished we could still get the treasure, so I snatched it before it went under with you."

"That is so much bilge!" laughed Captain Blade. "Fernando tried to save you, of course, but your hand slipped from his grasp and he only got the map. Luckily, Harry fished you out."

Sam's teeth were beginning to chatter with cold. "Th-th-thanks!" was all he could manage.

"We'll have you out of the water before you can say treasure," said Blade, wading downstream. "The river disappears into the ground just beyond here."

Soon they were climbing onto dry rock. They hugged themselves, trying to warm up, and took turns to hold their hands near the lantern flames.

"We must get moving," ordered Blade. "Sam'll freeze if we stay still."

They carried along the winding tunnel

and into a small echoing cave with one exit. Charlie stopped and looked all around.

"Sinbad's tunnel might have led him here," she said. "There are little holes all over the wall. Sinbad!" she called. "Here, puss. Here, boy."

She listened, but there was no answering miaow.

Harry and the captain made for the next passage with Fernando. Charlie hung back and clutched Sam's sleeve.

"I'm going back to look for Sinbad," she whispered. "He'll never find us if we walk any further." Sam could hear the panic in her voice.

"You can't," he whispered back. "You'll be in the dark and you'll have to face the river again."

"I don't care!" sobbed Charlie, running towards the tunnel they'd just left. "I'm not leaving him on his own in this terrible—"

A sudden rumbling filled the cave. Charlie froze, her eyes wide with fear. The rumbling grew louder. Sharp cracking sounds forked across the roof.

Then a noise like a massive explosion shook them from head to foot. Sam felt it go right through him, rattling his bones. Rocks began to rain down. Sam made a lunge for Charlie and dragged her into the tunnel where the others had gone. Behind them, huge chunks of the roof came thudding to the ground, filling the air with dust.

Sam could feel shards of stone striking his back as they raced blindly down the passage, towards the bobbing lantern lights.

"Are you two all right?" gasped Fernando when they skidded to a halt, coughing and choking in the dusty air.

Sam nodded and looked along the route they'd come. All he could see was a wall of rubble.

Their way out had disappeared.

"By Orion's bow!" cried Captain Blade. "That was a near thing."

"I knew I should have burnt that map!" exclaimed Harry Hopp, wiping the dust from his eyes. "We wouldn't be in this mess now if I had."

Captain Blade held up the lantern. "And we wouldn't be on the trail of treasure if you had," he said.

"Treasure's of little use to us now we're imprisoned here till we die!" muttered Harry.

"That can't be right," said Sam, feverishly looking at the map. "There must be a different way we can use to get out." He followed the spidery route across the parchment to the treasure cave. No matter how closely he looked at the faded ink, there seemed to be just the one way in and out. He could sense that everyone was holding their breath, waiting for his answer. "I can't find another," he said at last, in a small voice.

They were trapped deep underground, with no chance of rescue. Sam could almost feel the walls pressing in on him as he tried to fight down his panic.

"We won't take long to perish," muttered Fernando. "We've no food – and little water."

Harry suddenly slapped his belt. "The water bottles," he gasped, "and the sacks. They've gone. They must have got washed away in that river when I rescued Sam. We're doomed."

"Belay that talk!" said Blade firmly. "We find the booty and then look for another way out. And if we don't find one, we'll dig ourselves free with our bare hands. Onwards, my bold band."

Sam looked back down the tunnel to

where the rockfall blocked their exit from floor to roof. Even with shovels and a digger it would take days to shift it. But if the captain thought they could do it, then he knew they'd give it their best shot.

Blade led the way with Harry and Fernando close behind.

"Sinbad will never find us now!" wailed Charlie.

Sam didn't say anything, but he was beginning to think that Charlie was right.

The tunnel was low and narrow. It suddenly plunged downwards in rocky ledges, like giant steps.

"We're going into the bowels of the earth," murmured Fernando, as he clambered awkwardly down, his lantern swinging wildly. "What devilish things will we find there?"

"Remember those Indians we met up

Mexico way, Captain?" said Harry Hopp, reaching out a hand to help Charlie.

"Aye," grunted Blade, wriggling beneath a low overhang of jagged rock.

"They believed that all caves were the entrance to some horrible world called the Place of Fright," the first mate went on. "I've got a feeling in me gut that that's where we're headed."

The captain gave a hearty laugh. "And I've got a feeling in my gut that we're headed for a mound of treasure. I'd tell you all to hold your heads up – if it didn't mean you'd bash them on this roof— Aaghh!" He gave a sudden cry as he slipped forwards and disappeared.

Scrabbling vainly for handholds, the others found themselves sliding after him, bumping into each other in a headlong tumble. Sam heard the smash of lantern glass and they were plunged into darkness.

Sam landed heavily and rolled across a bumpy floor. He floundered about, trying to sit up. There were loose stick-like things all over the place that crunched as he moved, and his foot knocked against something round and hard that rolled away with a clatter. He could hear the groans of his shipmates close by.

"I have one of the lanterns and the candle's still inside," came Fernando's voice at last. There was a scrape of flint and a flash of flame and the cave was bathed in a dim glow.

Tattered shirts and breeches lay strewn across the floor.

"Why would anyone leave their clothes here?" asked Harry Hopp.

"They didn't," whispered Sam. He could see something gleaming in the flickering candlelight. "They're still in them."

Everyone stared dumbstruck at the ground. Human bones were protruding from the rotted cloth.

"By heaven!" muttered the captain at last, taking the lantern. "This place is awash with skeletons."

*And I've just played football with a skull,* Sam thought in horror, looking at the bony head that lay on its side, the jaw open in a huge yawn.

"This is why no one ever comes out of the Caves of Cocoza," said Fernando grimly. "They all die here in this terrible cavern."

# CHAPTER EIGHT

Captain Blade stood looking at the bones for a moment, a grim expression on his face. Then he turned to his shipmates.

"*They* may have perished," he said fiercely, "but we will not." He picked his way round the ghastly remains towards three dark slits in the wall. "We'll soon be far from this graveyard – if Sam can tell us which of these tunnels to take."

"It's the biggest one," said Sam. "The other two are dead ends. And the next cave has the treasure in it!"

"Then what are we waiting for?" declared Harry Hopp. "I'm happy to say farewell to our grinning friends."

They made good speed, eager to leave the bones behind. The narrow passage was easy to walk along but it seemed to lead on and on, curving round in a long arc.

"When are we ever going to reach the treasure?" demanded Harry, bending to avoid low needles of rock.

"I don't know," replied Sam anxiously. "It looks a lot straighter on the map."

The tunnel suddenly came to an end and Captain Blade held the lantern high. "Aha!" he exclaimed. "I think we've reached our goal."

They all crowded in, eager to see a dazzling display of jewels ready for the taking.

"I don't believe it!" exclaimed Fernando, staring in shock at the bones strewn across the ground.

"We're back at the same place!" gasped Charlie. "How could that have happened? Sinbad will be looking for us and we're just going round in circles."

"That tunnel twisted all over the place," groaned Harry. "Can we be sure we haven't happened upon a different cave of skeletons?"

"It's the same one, all right," said the captain, bitterly. "I remember that belt with the tarnished buckle."

The pirates stared wearily at the scattered bones they had hoped never to see again.

"This doesn't make sense!" exclaimed Sam. "We've just come out through one of the tunnels that the map said was a dead end." He looked at his shipmates in horror. "I don't know which way to go now."

The skulls seemed to grin at the pirates in evil delight, as if they had tricked them into coming back to this horrible place.

Harry Hopp threw himself to the ground with an angry *harrumph!*, scattering bones all about. "Stap me! This quest will be the death of us," he growled.

"Could you have read the map wrong, lad?" asked Blade.

Sam held the map under the lantern light, staring at the worm-like lines of the tunnels. Charlie looked over his shoulder. "We haven't gone wrong," he said at last. "But maybe there's something I missed. The ink's quite faint . . ."

He brought the map up closer and scrutinised every detail. Then he turned it over.

Charlie sighed. "There's nothing to help us on the back – a few more wiggly lines, that's all. Some sort of decoration."

"Throw it away," sighed Harry. "I don't want it in my sight."

But Sam just knew that this map was important. He knelt on the cave floor, smoothed it out and scrutinised it one last time. It didn't make any sense. Somehow it had to lead to the treasure if you were clever enough to work out how. He turned it over and studied the curious broken lines on the back. Why were they there?

"Wait a minute," said Charlie. "What's

that? I can see pairs of letters in the four corners."

"*R, E*," Sam read aloud. "Then there's an *E, A . . . T, R . . .* an *S* and a *U*."

"If you mix them up, they spell *treasure!*" said Charlie. "But that doesn't help. We know it's meant to be a treasure map already. Why put the letters in the corners like that?"

"If you bring them together you can read the word easily," said Sam. He folded the corners into the middle to show her. The letters came together to form *treasure*, written

in a circle. And, all at once, every squiggly line that had seemed like a meaningless pattern now joined up with others.

Sam couldn't believe what he was seeing.

"It's the real map of the caves!" he exclaimed. "The treasure is in the middle!"

"So whoever hid the treasure in here drew a false map," said Charlie, "and put the true one on the back."

"So no one else would find the way to it," added Fernando. "Very clever."

Sam leapt up and ran over to the third tunnel entrance. "This way to the treasure!"

"I'm right behind you!" said Harry Hopp, heaving himself up and following.

Sam let Fernando take the lead, lighting the way for the others.

"This path is leading upwards again," said Blade cheerfully. "We can forget all about your Place of Fright, Harry."

The way twisted on through the rock,

growing narrower and narrower. Sam began to worry. It seemed to be dwindling away to a dead end.

At last Fernando brought them to a halt. The pirates stared in dismay at what looked like a sheer wall. Sam groaned inwardly. Was this second map a false one too? Had they reached the end of their journey?

# CHAPTER NINE

The pirates looked at each other in the flickering light.

"Now where?" asked Harry Hopp.

"I don't know," said Sam, gulping down his fear.

A sudden miaow echoed all around them.

"Sinbad!" gasped Charlie. "He must be trapped somewhere and trying to get to us. I'll find you, puss!" She felt frantically round the walls. "Where is he?"

"I'll tell you where he is," said Harry. "There's someone sharpening his claws on my wooden leg!"

Charlie gave a whoop of delight. "Sinbad!" she cried happily, scooping up the scrawny ship's cat and showering his ragged ears with kisses. "You found us! Clever boy! And you're dry. You didn't come through the river."

"What did I tell you?" said Fernando, grinning. "He's one shipmate that never gets lost."

"But how did he get here?" asked Blade, as Sinbad glowered at the rest of the crew. "It's as if he came out of nowhere."

"He must have found a way," cried Sam. He inspected the wall but all he found was solid rock with a jutting ledge that threw a deep shadow to the ground. He bent down, running his hands over the cold stone. As he felt under the ledge his fingers slipped into nothing. "Bring the lantern here, Captain," he said in excitement. "There's a gap but it's not very wide."

"It'll be wide enough," declared the captain. "You young 'uns go first. Then Harry. He might need a bit of a push!"

Harry patted his belly. "Stap me!" he said with a chuckle. "I don't want to get stuck now – I can almost smell that treasure!"

Fernando disappeared into the dark hole. Sam and Charlie followed. The captain passed the lantern to them and Harry began to squeeze himself into the gap.

"This hole's smaller than I thought," he panted. "In fact, I believe it may be too small for—"

He gave a yelp of pain and suddenly
shot through to land at their feet.

"Are you all right, Mr Hopp?" asked
Charlie anxiously. "You came out like a
cork from a bottle!"

"Aye," growled Harry, rubbing his shin.
His leg was scratched and bleeding. "That
Sinbad gave me a bit of encouragement."

The ship's cat stalked out of the hole,
tail held high. Captain Blade chuckled as
he joined them. "Sinbad thought you

were going a bit too slowly. Now, where are we?"

They gazed round the cave, eagerly searching for signs of the booty. The lantern threw the clefts in the wall into deep shadow. They could see bats clustered on the roof, between glistening stalactites. Stalagmites as thick as tree trunks rose from the ground, making odd knobbly sculptures. The largest nearly reached the ceiling. Its top was covered in small peaks, like the points of a crown.

Harry Hopp took the lantern from Fernando and began searching the cave. "I can't see a single pearl or gold coin anywhere," he grunted. "This treasure must be well hidden."

Sinbad scrambled up the tallest stalagmite and peered back down at them between the points of the crown, his eyes large and shining in the lantern light. Then he reached out a paw and batted something to the edge. It glistened as it tumbled down towards them.

Fernando caught it. "It's a brooch!" he exclaimed, holding it up for everyone to see. "And it's covered in rubies. Sinbad's found the treasure!"

"Shiver me timbers, so he has," declared Harry Hopp, as Sinbad leapt down into Charlie's arms. "That's some hiding place!"

The captain turned to Sam. "You got us this far, lad," he said, "so you can go first to see our riches."

Sam didn't waste a second. While the crew waited eagerly at the bottom, he hauled himself up the slippery stalagmite and plunged his hand into the deep dark hollow at the top.

His fingers touched necklaces, rings and more brooches. Underneath he could feel plates, candlesticks and bags of coins. He pulled out a goblet and held it up for the others to see.

"Pure gold!" sighed Harry Hopp, his eyes fixed on the jewel-encrusted cup that sparkled in the lantern light.

Sam gave a loud whoop of delight. Immediately a flurry of bats took off from the cave roof and swirled round, squeaking anxiously.

"Oh, no, you don't," Charlie told Sinbad, who was struggling to free himself so he could try to catch one. "This time you're staying with us!"

When the bats had settled, hanging upside down from the rock crevices, Sam passed down the booty.

"It's not a huge hoard," said Fernando, admiring an intricate gold earring, "but I'd swear it's very valuable."

"We have you to thank for this find, Sam," said Blade, feasting his eyes on the sight. "You worked out the trick of the map. Fernando is right. This haul is incredibly valuable. These precious pieces will help us arm the *Sea Wolf* to the gunnels."

"With finer weapons than we've ever dreamed of," agreed Fernando.

"And we'll have a great banquet!" added Charlie.

"Not cooked by Peter!" put in Harry

with a chuckle. He picked up some bags of coins and hung them on his belt. "Sooner we get this lot stowed, the sooner we can leave this place. We didn't need those sacks after all."

It wasn't long before every pocket was heaving with coins and the pirates were festooned with bracelets and necklaces.

"Now to see if there's a way out," said Sam. He spotted a hole high in the wall. He could see some bats hanging just inside the entrance. "That could be the route Sinbad took to reach this cave, but it looks too small for us. I'll check the map for another one."

"Good plan!" exclaimed Harry. "There's no hope of me getting through that."

"And we can't go back the way we came because of that horrible rockfall," said Charlie.

Sam was holding the parchment under the lantern. There was no sign of the narrow passage in the wall, but there was something else. "Awesome!" he cried. "I mean . . . stap me! There's a really easy route leading out from here. It takes us straight back to where our path first forked.

"Where is this route?" asked the captain.

"According to the map there's a tunnel opposite where we came in!" Sam said.

"I've found it!" called Fernando, pointing with a hand covered in rings. "This way to freedom!"

"We hardly need a light, men," laughed Captain Blade, as they marched along, chinking loudly. "We make so much noise that we'll never lose each other!"

"It's a shame we didn't know about this way to the treasure," said Harry Hopp. "We'd have saved ourselves a deal of trouble."

"But it was worth it in the end," said Captain Blade. "A hard battle brings a greater victory."

"Not sure about that," huffed Harry. "I'd have been just as happy if that scoundrel had poured this lot into my lap at the tavern."

"Here's the place where we took the other fork," said Fernando. "We'll be back on the *Sea Wolf* and off with our gold before you can say Caves of Cocoza."

"There's sunlight ahead!" cried Charlie happily. "We've made it."

Half running, half stumbling in their

haste, they burst out into the clean sea
air.

"All aboard the rowing boat," said Blade.
"It's time to show our crewmates—"

"Stop right there!" came a voice from
above them.

They froze. Sam craned his neck to look
up at the cliff face over the entrance. He
caught his breath in surprise.

Scammell was perched on a rock, a nasty grin on his face and a flintlock pistol pointed at them. Even his false eye seemed to be mocking them. A group of men were crouched at his side. They had knives and cutlasses in their hands.

"Congratulations, Mr Hopp," said Scammell. "You and your friends 'ave succeeded where no one else ever has."

# CHAPTER TEN

S am gulped. Scammell's unblinking false
eye seemed to bore right through them.

"We have found the treasure, and what's
that to you?" growled Harry Hopp, his
fists clenching.

"Everything," said Scammell. He gave
the captain a ragged salute. "When I heard
you were from the *Sea Wolf* it gave me an
idea. If anyone could survive the Caves of

Cocoza, then I was sure Captain Blade and 'is brave crew could. Well done to you all. And you come out looking like the richest monarchs in the world."

"We thank you for your words," said Blade. "And now we'll bid you farewell."

"Not so fast!" snapped the villain, raising his gun. "You will 'and the booty over to me and maybe I'll let you live." He aimed the gun at the captain's chest. "Or maybe I won't."

He clicked his fingers and one of his men came forwards with a sack. The others jumped down in front of the *Sea Wolf* crewmates and ripped the jewels and bags of coins from them.

Charlie held grimly onto Sinbad with one hand and flung her gems to the ground with the other. Sam hoped she could keep him from attacking the enemy. One move from any of the *Sea Wolf* crew and the villains would shoot.

"I knew I should have killed you there and then," growled Harry Hopp.

"That's why I didn't gave you the chance," said Scammell smoothly. "There were no governor's men in town — it was just Alf 'ere raising the alarm to give me a chance to escape."

"You miserable wretch!" stormed Harry.

"Belay that, Mr Hopp!" said Captain Blade in a warning tone.

"We were cunning when we came after you, too," the rogue went on with a sly grin. "We were just one more ship sailing along in the distance, minding our own business."

Sam felt fury rising in his chest. Hadn't he done his job properly? Should he have known that they were being followed? Then he had a terrible thought. The *Sea Wolf* was waiting at the mouth of the inlet. These men would have had to get past her to reach the cave entrance. They must have out-fought his shipmates on their way.

"What have you done to the rest of our crew?" he burst out.

Scammell burst into evil laughter. "Ignorant boy! You don't think we'd waste time cutting them to pieces. We anchored on the other side of the island and came overland." He tapped his forehead and his false eye seemed to see right inside Sam's brain. "We're clever, see."

"Cowardly, more like," said Charlie through gritted teeth. "You'd all be dead if you'd met our shipmates in a fight."

One of the captors raised a hand to cuff her, but then leapt back hurriedly to avoid Sinbad's swiping claws.

The man with the sack raised it and gave it a shake. "This be the sum total of what they're carrying," he reported.

"It doesn't look a lot now it's been put together," said their leader, narrowing his one good eye in suspicion. "I can't believe that this little haul is all there is to the fabled Treasure of Cocoza. Tell me what you've done with the rest before I slit your throats."

"We couldn't carry everything," Sam burst out. His crewmates stared at him in surprise. But Sam knew what he was doing. If the false-eyed scoundrel believed that there was more treasure to be found, he wouldn't rest till he'd got it and he'd be too busy to think about slitting throats. A plan was forming in Sam's head. He'd offer to lead the way straight to more booty – well, that's what the villains would *think* he was doing. In fact, he'd take them the longest way he could to the empty treasure cave and then escape along the quick exit route, leaving them inside to try and follow the long, winding tunnels back. He'd need a diversion though. Something to grab their attention while he slipped off back to his crewmates.

*Merow!* Sinbad was struggling in Charlie's

arms and that gave Sam the idea he needed. When they reached the treasure cave, he'd disturb the bats just like the ship's cat had done. While the villains were blinded by the flapping wings, he'd slip away and join his friends. They'd be back on their ship while Scammell and his men were still trying to get out. Even though the *Sea Wolf* crew wouldn't have the treasure, at least they'd be alive. Whatever Scammell might say, Sam was sure he meant to kill them.

"There's loads more gold in there," he went on. "I'll show you where it is. We would have brought it out but we couldn't carry it all."

He could see that his crewmates were still looking puzzled, and Sam couldn't tell them what he was up to. He hoped they wouldn't say anything. Scammell had to believe his story for the plan to work.

"This is a trick!" the villain began. "You can't fool me with your—"

But suddenly Captain Blade reached out and cuffed Sam round the head.

"You bilge-swilling barnacle!" he roared. "What did you tell them that for? There's a king's ransom in there. We were going to go back for it ourselves — and you're the only one who understands that cursed map."

Sam's heart leapt. The blow hadn't hurt a bit. The captain had realised that Sam had a plan and he was playing along.

"I don't care about you lot any more," he told Blade, curling his lip in the nastiest sneer he could manage. "I reckon this is my only chance of staying alive."

"Traitor!" Charlie muttered under her breath.

Sam was pretty sure she was just joining in with the pretence, but she sounded really angry. He turned his back on his shipmates. He had to hope they understood what he was doing.

Scammell rubbed his calloused hands together in evil delight. "We'll get rid of these snivelling fools first," he said. "We've no further use for them. It'll be a pleasure to dispatch the famous Captain Blade and his minions — as slowly as possible."

Sam was horrified. His plan was going very wrong. Scammell was going to kill his crewmates!

"Why don't you wait till we get back?" he said quickly.

"Whose side are you on?" growled Scammell, bringing his gun up hard under Sam's throat. "Don't you want to see them die?"

"Of course I do," answered Sam
earnestly. "I just don't think we should
stop to do it right this minute. It's very
dangerous in there," he went on. "We set
off with twenty-four men! But there were
rockfalls and floods and we are the only
survivors. We need to go now while we can
still reach the treasure cave."

Scammell moved back and Sam thought
he'd won him over, but the villain slid a
sharp knife out of his belt and tested the
blade with a thumb.

Sam's stomach lurched. "There's so
much wealth in there that you'll be rich

for life," he urged. "You don't want to lose time over a few miserable buccaneers."

"You're a treacherous sea slug, Sam!" cried Harry. "I was counting on getting that chest of doubloons for myself – though the roof did look very unsafe there." Sam had to stop himself from smiling. The first mate was in on the act, too!

"Very well then," agreed Scammell, reluctantly putting away the knife. "It'll give me a better chance to come up with a really painful end for them." He turned on the captive pirates with a sneer. "And, while we're gone, you can be thinking about just what that end might be."

His comrades let out vicious laughs and slapped each other on the back. Scammell picked up a lantern. "Alf and Zeke, stay and keep a close eye on the prisoners." He threw them each a gun from his belt. "And keep the treasure safe. You know what 'appens to those that double-cross me!"

Sam glanced over to his shipmates. They were giving him grateful looks. *They know I've saved their lives,* Sam thought in relief. *For the time being, anyway.*

Scammell grabbed him roughly by the jerkin. "One wrong move," he pulled a finger slowly across Sam's throat, "and you're *dead.*"

# CHAPTER ELEVEN

Sam led the way into the caves. He strode purposefully along, trying not to show the fear that was creeping over him. He was going deep underground with a bunch of desperate men. If his plan didn't work, Scammell would show him no mercy.

The false-eyed villain and his crew followed closely, jostling Sam along in the tunnels. They came to the first fork, where Sam knew that the right-hand passage would take them straight to the treasure cave. Instead, he started to head towards the left.

"'old 'ard!" snarled Scammell, grasping his arm roughly. "What's wrong with the other way?"

Sam paused and put on the saddest expression he could manage. "It leads to a sheer drop," he said in a low mournful voice. "Poor Ned. He didn't stand a chance."

"Left it is then," muttered Scammell.

The men complained bitterly as the going got harder and Sam felt their angry stares burn into his back.

When they reached the next place where the path divided, Sam was about to lead the band down the tunnel he and his shipmates had taken, but then he remembered the landslide blocking the path. He made a show of standing under a lantern to study the false map. Then he folded the corners together as if he was putting it away and secretly glanced at the real route that was now revealed. To his relief he saw another route that led to the cave of bones. That was the way they'd go. The villains deserved to be scared by the skeletons.

The passages were narrow and winding and seemed to go on for ever. Finally the pirates piled into the cave of bones.

"Damn your kidneys!" cried Scammell as skeletal fingers crunched under his foot. "You've brought us into Hell." He whipped out his knife and pressed it into Sam's jerkin, close to his heart. "Are you mocking us, lad? These dead men don't look like they went the right way. You wouldn't be taking us away from the true path, would you?"

Sam felt as if spiders were scuttling about inside his stomach. He realised that the false-eyed scoundrel was losing patience fast. "Why would I do that?" he said quickly. "I want the rest of this hoard as much as you. You have to trust me. These dead men didn't have a map." He looked at the frightened faces of Scammell's crew. "I hope your lot are braver than some of ours were. The sight of the bones drove Ben and Peter mad. We haven't seen the lily-livered cowards since."

Scammell turned his knife on his men. "Any coward gets my blade in his gizzard."

*Got away with that!* thought Sam in relief. *Let's hope my luck holds when I try to escape!*

"Not far to the treasure cave now," he said brightly, pointing the way. "It's narrow but it's the only way to the treasure."

The men were off, eager to leave the bones behind. Sam walked after them, Scammell at his back. Soon he heard puffs and groans as they all squeezed through the narrow gap to the cave.

Sam followed. Now they were in the treasure cave, he'd carry out the rest of his plan. *Wait a minute!* he thought in alarm.

The cave didn't look the same. Where was the exit tunnel that they'd found? The far wall was just a huge pile of rubble. Had he lost his way, after all, and brought the men to the wrong place? But there was the lumpy stalagmite where they'd found the treasure – and, suddenly, Sam realised what had happened. There had been a rockfall since he and his friends had been here. The exit tunnel was blocked. *Now* what was he going to do?

"Well," growled Scammell, "what are you waiting for? Which way do we go?"

"I'm just trying to remember," answered Sam, frowning and looking around the craggy walls for another escape route. "I have to get it right . . ."

To his dismay, all he could see was the small opening that he thought Sinbad had used to get to the treasure cave. There was nothing else for it. He would have to try and escape that way. It wasn't on the map — and he couldn't be sure it would be wide enough for him — but it was his only hope! He just had to disturb the bats first so no one would see him go.

Could he throw something at them? But the false-eyed rogue was watching him closely, his hand on the hilt of his knife. Sam couldn't move.

"Tell me the way *now!*" demanded Scammell.

And then Sam had it. An idea zoomed into his brain as fast as a cannonball. He'd send the whole band of them up to disturb the bats! He pointed to the top of the stalagmite column. "Up there," he said. "There's an opening in the ceiling. It leads to the treasure cave. Those bats are covering it but they'll move if you make enough noise."

"At them, men!" bellowed Scammell
and his crew scrambled up the stalagmite,
waving their arms and yelling at the tops
of their voices.

The bats took off from the ceiling in a
flurry of high-pitched squeals. The cave
was instantly full of black flapping wings.
Scammell and his men were surrounded,
flailing their arms in terror. A man near
him dropped his lantern in surprise and

Sam snatched it before the candle could go out. He grasped the lantern handle in his teeth and was soon climbing up towards his escape route, groping for finger- and toe-holds as he went. He hauled himself into the tunnel, disturbing more bats that had settled inside. They fluttered about his face and then flew off.

Sam slid into the small gap until his feet were out of sight and then lay there panting and listening to the frightened shouts below. He stared into the gloom ahead, his stolen lantern giving only a

feeble light. What was he going to do if the tunnel *was* too small for him? But if he didn't go forwards he'd have to go back — and Scammell and his men now knew that he'd tricked them. They wouldn't exactly throw a party for him if he popped up again.

The narrow tunnel was his only way out.

# CHAPTER TWELVE

Sam began to crawl along the rough tunnel. The distant voices of the pirates echoed round him. They had turned from frightened to angry now — they knew he had gone! Soon they'd be trying to find their way out of the caves. Sam had to hope that he got out first.

He moved along as fast as he could, the lantern swinging in front of him. He grazed his knees and elbows as he went and nearly yelled as his head suddenly hit the rock above. The passage was getting lower. Sam flattened himself onto his stomach and inched along. Supposing there was another rockfall, or this was the wrong tunnel! He hadn't actually *seen* the cat come out of it. Perhaps Sinbad had found another route. Images of being trapped for ever in this terrible underground prison kept finding their way into his head. He pushed the thoughts away.

Suddenly he could hear faint, high-pitched whistles. He must be coming to the bats' cave. This *was* the way Sinbad had come. Soon Sam was jumping eagerly down from the hole where Sinbad had first disappeared and into the familiar cave. He skirted round the stalagmites and plunged into the passageway opposite. At last he crept into the shadows of the cave on the shore. He stopped and blew out his lantern. It was time to rescue his shipmates.

Sam crouched down behind the rocks at the entrance. He could see Alf and Zeke standing guard, cutlasses in their hands, and, just beyond, his friends sitting on the ground. Charlie was gripping Sinbad tightly to stop him from attacking. Long evening shadows fell on them. Sam shifted his position. Now he could just make out his crewmates' weapons, thrown in a pile. They lay between him and the guards. If only he could get to them.

"They've been gone a long time," muttered Alf.

Zeke threw a glance towards the cave entrance. Sam shrank back into the gloom. "Yeah," he said, scratching his head. "They'd better hurry up. We'll want to catch the next tide."

"I reckon they're lost in the caves," said Alf.

"Nah!" said Zeke. "They've got the boy and the map. They'll be out soon. And I'm not budging till we're holding that treasure in our hands."

"Then you'll be here a long time!" sneered Alf. "I'll tell you what's happened. The guardians of the caves have got them – and that boy, too." Alf waved his gun at the hostages. "I say we kill these snivelling fools, take what treasure we have in the sack and go now, before nightfall."

"And I say we stay," insisted Zeke obstinately. "Mr Scammell will keelhaul us if we go — especially if we steal the booty."

Alf grinned at his shipmate. "Then there's only one way to settle it." Sam saw him delve into the pouch on his belt. "We toss a coin. If the crest's on top we stay, if it's the lion we go."

"And take the prisoners with us?" asked Zeke.

"Of course not!" said Alf. "We'll get rid of them first."

Zeke's sulky face broke into a grin. "Good idea. If I lose, at least I'll get the pleasure of a spot of killing."

"And there's nothing we like better," agreed Alf nastily.

 Sam held his breath as Alf put the coin on his finger and thumb and spun it high in the air.

He caught it in his palm and slapped it onto the back of his hand. He looked over at Sam's crewmates with a twisted smile. "The lion," he smirked. "Bad luck, me hearties. We're off to our ship — and you're all going to die."

# CHAPTER THIRTEEN

Alf and Zeke raised their pistols.
Sam didn't have time to stop and
think. He burst out of the cave with a
bloodcurdling war cry.

The two villains spun round in alarm.
In an instant their guns were aiming at
Sam's heart. Sam had saved his friends
but now he was the target instead. There
was nowhere to hide. He could only wait

to feel the bullets whipping through his body.

As Alf and Zeke pulled their triggers, Harry Hopp and Fernando flung themselves at their backs, sending them sprawling. Before Alf could struggle to his feet, Sinbad leapt on his chest with a terrifying yowl. The man froze in terror. Fernando and Charlie snatched up their cutlasses and held them at his throat. Zeke's pistol had spun from his hands, far away over the rocks. Cursing, he drew his sword, swung round and leapt towards Captain Blade. Sam gave a cry of horror. He was too far away to defend his captain – but there was one thing he *could* do. He seized a cutlass and sent it spinning through the air towards the captain. Blade caught it expertly and, in one fluid move, he was fighting back.

"Stop now and I'll spare your life," said the captain pleasantly as he deflected

a sword thrust and went on the attack.

In an instant the sharp point of the
captain's sword was at Zeke's throat. Zeke
held his hands up in front of him. Harry
got some rope from the rowing boat, sat
their two guards back to back on the shore
and tied them firmly together.

"Have you still got the map, Sam?"

asked Blade. Sam delved inside his pocket and handed over the tattered paper. The captain tossed it near Zeke's feet. "Here," he growled. "When you've got yourselves free you can use this to find your friends."

Zeke glanced over at the cave entrance with a look of horror. "We'll never find our way if we venture in there," he said.

Blade gave a shrug. "That's your choice."

Harry Hopp scooped up the sack of treasure. "I believe this is ours," he said cheerfully. "I always said it was a good idea to come to the Caves of Cocoza!"

He gave a huge belly laugh and everybody joined in. They were still chuckling as they rowed back to their ship.

The *Sea Wolf* cut through the waves, her
sails filled with wind and her snarling
wolf's-head flag gleaming in the sun.
The crew clustered round to admire the
treasure.

"Pieces of eight!" squawked Crow,
landing on Sam's shoulder and nibbling his
ear.

"The parrot . . . I mean, the crow is
right," said Ned, with a quick glance at
Captain Blade to see if he'd noticed his
mistake. "It's a fine haul."

"Aye," said the captain, holding up a ring
with a green stone. "This alone is worth a
king's ransom."

"That villain was too stupid to see
it," said Harry Hopp. "Though we can
excuse him, since he only had the one
eye!"

"I wonder if they've found their way out yet," said Sam. He shuddered at the thought of being lost deep underground. But at least Blade had given Scammell and his men some sort of chance to get out.

Fernando gave a grim chuckle. "I doubt Alf and Zeke are trying to help them."

"I bet they've run away," agreed Charlie. She rubbed Sinbad under his chin. The scruffy ship's cat stretched his neck, his eyes shut in ecstasy. "Who's a clever boy?" she crooned.

"He is," said Sam. "If it hadn't been for him going after the bats, I'd still be in those horrible caves." Without thinking, he reached out a hand to stroke Sinbad.

*Merow!* Hissing, the cat was on his feet. In the nick of time, Sam got his fingers out of the way of Sinbad's vicious claws.

"Enemy attack!" screeched Crow, flapping up to the top of the mast. Sinbad chased him as far as the first yardarm, then sat and began to give himself a thorough clean.

"Set course for Skeleton Island!" said Captain Blade, making for the wheel. "We've got treasure to stow away." He stopped and turned to Ben. "But first break out the rum. Double rations for all. We're celebrating!"

The crew cheered. Sam joined in, wondering how he could avoid drinking the horrible stuff without upsetting the rest of his shipmates.

He felt a tingling in his fingers and toes and realised that he wouldn't have to worry about the rum after all. His magic gold doubloon was taking him back to his own time.

"I'm going to have a quick nap first," he blurted as he ran for the steps that led to the gun deck. He had to be out of sight before he disappeared. Even if his shipmates drank a barrel of rum, they'd never believe it if he vanished in front of their eyes.

He'd just made it to the storeroom when he was swept up in the dark whirlwind that took him forwards through the centuries. All was black for a second and then he landed with a thump on his bedroom carpet. Sam grinned to himself as he dropped his doubloon into the old bottle on his shelf. His teacher was

going to love reading his homework! He'd
now got a fantastic story to write, full of
treasure and villains and plenty of danger.
Miss Elliott would think he'd invented it
all – little did she know that undercover
pirates were always having top-secret,
swashbuckling adventures!

# CREW MANIFEST

Sinbad

Crow

Thomas Blade
Captain

Peter Craddock
Ship's Cook

Fernando
Rigger

Don't miss the next exciting adventure in the
*Sam Silver: Undercover Pirate* series

# THE SEA MONSTER

Available in October 2013!
Read on for a special preview
of the first two chapters.

# Chapter One

Sam Silver raced up the high street of Backwater Bay and skidded through the door of his parents' fish and chip shop.

"I'm home!" he yelled as he sped past his mother and up to their flat on the first floor. He was too busy to stop and chat. He was on a mission. It had been a long hard day of spellings and maths at school and he'd promised himself an exciting pirate adventure to help him recover.

His friends had exciting pirate adventures by reading about them in books or playing computer games, but Sam had an amazing secret. He'd found a magic coin that could whisk him off to join Captain Blade's crew on board the *Sea Wolf*, a pirate ship from over three hundred years ago. And the great thing was that when he was back in 1706, looking for treasure and fighting sea battles, not one second went by in the present – so no one missed him.

Since his mum would definitely notice if he got his school uniform blown up by cannonballs or nibbled by sharks, Sam always wore an old T-shirt and jeans on his time travels. He pulled his drawer open to find them and stopped in horror. Normally they were crumpled up at the

back behind his socks. Today they were lying neatly folded right on top. And what was worse — they'd been washed and ironed!

Sam had a horrible sinking feeling, as if someone had pulled a plug in his tummy. It would be bad enough wearing clean clothes on a pirate ship, but he'd suddenly remembered that he'd left his magic doubloon in his jeans. He'd taken the coin from the bottle on his shelf to set off on an adventure last night, when his mum had appeared at his bedroom door. He'd quickly shoved the coin into his pocket and that's where it was now. At least he hoped so. Suppose it had been washed out of his jeans and into the water to disappear for ever down the drain?

Frantically he searched, turning his trousers inside-out and shaking them hard. Nothing. He was never going to see his buccaneer friends again.

Then he realised he'd missed the tiny pocket under the waistband. He pushed two fingers in – it was empty. The washing machine had eaten his precious coin! Wait a minute. What about the time he'd left a football medal among his clothes? His mum had found it in the rubber bit round the door of the machine. Maybe that's where the doubloon would be! But as Sam raced into the kitchen he nearly fell over a man in overalls who was taking the washing machine apart.

Sam's face fell.

"It looks bad, doesn't it?" said the man cheerily. "This pipe's jammed. There's something stuck in it."

"What is it?" asked Sam.

"Not sure," said the man. "It's hard to tell with all the muck in there." He fed a rod down the pipe.

Sam held his breath. The man pulled out a lump of sludge and poked about in it. "Got it!" he said at last, holding up a dirty metal disk. "It's a coin — bit funny-looking though." He went to give it a wipe with a cloth.

"No!" cried Sam, scared that if the man rubbed it he'd be the one to disappear back to 1706. "It's mine," he added quickly. "Thanks. I'll take it."

Sam ran back to his room. He had to find out if his gold doubloon still worked. It wasn't meant to go through the wash! Its special power had probably been flushed away. He pulled on his horribly neat T-shirt and jeans. Then he spat on the coin and gave it a rub.

At once he was whooshed up inside a dark, spinning tunnel.

He'd been silly to think that the washing machine could have destroyed the magic. The coin just needed a bit of Silver spit and polish.

"*Sea Wolf*, here I come!" he yelled.

In an instant Sam found himself sprawled across the floor of a small room, surrounded by wooden barrels and coils of rope. Awesome! He was back in the storeroom on the *Sea Wolf*. The ship was swaying beneath his feet as he put on his jerkin, neckerchief and belt and picked up his spyglass. His friend Charlie always made sure they were left there for him. Charlie was the only member of the crew who knew he came from the twenty-first century. The others believed that each time he disappeared, he had just dashed off home to help his poor widowed mum on her farm. None of his shipmates thought this was odd, as pirates love their mothers more than anything else.

Sam stowed the coin safely in his pocket. Then he ran out of the storeroom and made for the deck, taking the steps in three bounds. The crew were busy splicing ropes, mending sails and climbing the rigging. They sang a cheerful sea shanty as they worked in the hot Caribbean sunshine. Sam could see Charlie helping Ned the bosun mend a broken piece of

the starboard rail. Ned swung his hammer in time to the song, joining in the chorus with a booming voice.

Captain Blade stood close by, peering at a map. He was pulling at the braids in his beard, deep in thought.

"Head south, shipmates," he ordered. "I warrant the French treasure galleons will be coming that way."

"Aye!" cried a stubbly-faced man with a wooden leg. He turned the ship's wheel to set the course. "And with this fair wind, we'll be meeting them before midday or my name's not Harry Hopp!"

*Excellent!* thought Sam. *I've got back just in time for a treasure hunt.*

"Mainsail all correct, Captain," came a cry from above his head and Fernando shot down the rigging, his hands and feet moving so fast they were a blur. "Do you want me on lookout now?"

"No need for that," called Sam, running to the middle of the deck. "*I'm* here and ready for duty in the crow's nest."

Fernando let out a Spanish exclamation and slapped Sam hard on the back, a huge grin on his face at the sight of his friend.

"Sam Silver!" declared the captain. "By Jupiter's chariot, how did you get to us a day's sail from land? You couldn't have swum that far!"

Sam was always so excited at being back on the *Sea Wolf* that he never remembered to think up how he might have got there.

If he said that he'd popped back from three hundred years in the future they'd think he'd lost his wits.

"He must have climbed aboard at Tortuga when we stopped for provisions," said Charlie, coming to his rescue as usual.

"That's right," said Sam, gratefully.

"We never saw you," said Harry Hopp, frowning.

"That's because . . ." Sam began, thinking furiously.

"That's because he was asleep in the hold," said Charlie. "He was snoring like a warthog. I'm surprised you didn't hear him!"

"I was exhausted by the time I got here," added Sam. "My mum wanted me to muck out the pigs and milk the goat before I left."

"What a dutiful son," said Harry.

"Your poor mother," added Ned the

bosun, wiping away a tear.
"Managing a whole farm
on her own."

"Well, I'm very
grateful she could
spare you," said
Captain Blade.
"Get up into that
crow's nest, lad. We
need you to keep a weather eye out for the
French ships laden with treasure!"

Sam didn't need telling twice. "Aye, aye,
Captain!" he cried happily.

# CHAPTER TWO

Sam had just started climbing the rigging when there was a flutter of green feathers and a parrot landed on the rope in front of him. It began chewing at the nearest knot.

"Hello, Crow," said Sam in delight. "What are you up to?"

"Take that pesky bird aloft with you!" yelled Ned, waving his hammer. "He's been mad hungry these past few days, gnawing at anything he could find. I've had to replace two chair legs and half the ship's rail!"

"But not before I'd sat on the chair and gone tumbling!" growled Harry Hopp. "That varmint will be after my wooden leg next."

"Don't be too hard on him," said Peter the cook. "You know he's been ill. He didn't eat for a week."

"That's because you fed him your oyster stew," said Charlie.

Crow turned his head on one side and peered at Sam. Then he flew onto his shoulder and began to nibble at his leather jerkin.

"Poor thing," said Sam, stroking his crest. "I know what's wrong," he told

the crew. "It's not that he's hungry. If he's been ill, his beak will have overgrown. Parrots' beaks grow all the time and they have to gnaw on wood and things to trim them. They don't gnaw when they feel unwell, so now Crow's got extra gnawing to do to get his beak back to normal."

"How do you know that?" asked Peter.

*Oops*, thought Sam. *I can't tell them I heard it on a school trip to the zoo.*

"My mum told me," he blustered. "She's got loads of parrots . . . on her farm."

Captain Blade shuddered. "Sounds like a terrible place."

The bold Captain Blade, who would fight ten men at one go, was scared stiff of parrots. Harry Hopp said it was because one of the feathered fiends had dive-bombed him in his crib, but all the pirates told a different tale about their leader's one fear.

Sam swung up the rigging, the parrot

gripping tightly to his shoulder. As he climbed over the side of the crow's nest, the parrot flapped onto the flagpole and started attacking it with his beak. Sam swept the horizon with his spyglass. On the port side a few ships were sailing by in the distance but none was flying the plain white French flag.

Sam looked to starboard. A single vessel seemed to be heading their way.

He checked the flag at the top of the mast. As the wind caught it he could make out a shark over a skull and crossbones.

"Pirate ship ahoy!" he yelled. "Dead ahead."

"Let's see if they want to share their booty with us, lads," cried Harry Hopp eagerly. "Get ready to 'persuade' them."

"I recognise that ship," reported Fernando. "It's the *Truro*."

But Sam had spotted something strange.

"What's happened to her?" he called

down. "The sails are flapping loose. There's no sign of life."

He heard the captain burst out laughing. "I think our crafty friends are trying to outwit us. They're pretending they've abandoned ship."

"And as soon as we get close they'll attack," warned Ned.

"Go carefully, men," ordered Harry. "We'll show them we're no fools."

The crew ran to man the cannon.

As they sailed closer to the ship, Sam saw that parts of the *Truro*'s hull had been smashed, the rigging was in shreds and the mizzen mast torn from the deck. "I don't think it's a trick!" he exclaimed. "Looks like she's had a fight and the men are gone."

"Shiver me timbers, the boy's right," agreed Harry in surprise. He shouted orders to the crew. "Go about and get alongside. There may still be some pickings for us."

The crew quickly tethered the two ships together and laid a plank bridge between them. Sam sped down the rigging and ran to the captain. "Permission to go aboard with the others, sir?" he asked.

Blade nodded. "Follow me," he commanded. "Weapons at the ready. This could still be a trick."

Ben Hudson, the quartermaster, threw Sam a cutlass and Sam climbed onto one of the planks after Blade. The sea churned far below. Being so high reminded him of

Monkey World at Backwater Bay, where you climbed tall trees and went down incredibly long zip wires — except that there were no helmets and safety ropes here. In fact, there was nothing between him and the ocean! Sam felt his legs tingle with terror and excitement.

He leapt onto the deck of the *Truro*. Charlie, Fernando and Ned followed, with other crew members close behind.

"Well, knock me down with a conker!" declared Ned. "This is a strange mess."

Knives and cutlasses lay scattered all over the place. Ben put his hand on a cannon. "Stone cold," he said. "I'd bet all the treasure in Trinidad that this hasn't been fired."

"I agree," said Captain Blade. "It looks as if there's been a fight but where are the bodies? Go carefully, shipmates."

Moving cautiously forwards, Sam noticed a dark liquid spattered over the boards and seeping into the wood. *Blood!* he thought with horror. Then he realised it was more black than red.

"Check this out," he told Charlie. They bent down to inspect it. "I think it's ink."

"That's odd," she replied. "Why would anyone spill ink in the middle of a battle? It's not the time to be writing letters!"

A terrified cry filled the air as a man leapt out from a hatch in the deck. Eyes wild in his pale face, he rounded on them

all, waving a broken oar. "Get away from me! I'll fight . . ." he quavered, his words tailing off as he stared at them. "I'll fight," he repeated with a sob.

"Is he mad?" asked Fernando.

The captain put his pistol in his belt and held out his hands towards the gibbering man. "It's Jem Plunkett, isn't it?" he said. "Ship's carpenter?"

"Aye," gasped Jem, collapsing in front of them, his makeshift weapon clattering down beside him.

Blade gripped his shoulder. "What's been going on here?" he asked. "Where is everyone?"

"Gone," croaked Jem. He looked round at them, horror all over his face. "They were taken." He gulped hard. "They were plucked from the ship like ants."

"He *is* crazed," declared Ned.

"No, I swear it," said the *Truro* pirate, clutching at the captain's sleeve. "It rose out of the waves and ate them in front of my very eyes!"

"What did?" asked Charlie in a frightened whisper.

"A huge sea monster."

# the
## orion star